MW00570982

Published by: QuickTurtle Books LLC®

https://www.booksmakebooms.com

ISBN: 978-1-940736-71-6

Published in the United States of America

Michigan Brown Trout Festival

Presents

Big Brownie

Richard Rensberry

Note:
There is a glossary
at the back of this book
for any unusual or difficult words.

Big Brownie

The fishermen came
with their boats and nets,
their flashy gold lures
and bravado big bets.

They scurried the dark
where the river ends,
boating huge coolers
with hollers to friends.

Big Brownie was tagged
and lurking the bay,
the reward on his head
the talk of the day.

With the wind dying down
the water lay slack.
Where the buoys pinged
it was foggy and black.

When the sun burned through
fish lines were set;
the planer boards hummed
in the wait and fret.

The day wore on
in pursuit of the quest;
the radios abuzz
wishing all the best.

Big Brownie was tagged
and lurking the bay,
the reward on his head
the talk of the day.

The boats straggled home
beneath a sky painted rust,
their hopes and pride
either buoyed or bust.

Leaderboard

Brown Trout- Ziltch Zero

King Salmon- Dennis Johnson 29 lbs

Lake Trout- William Reys 18 lbs

Walleye- Dave Polaski 9 lbs 5 oz

Atlantic Salmon- Keith Banyan 8 lbs

At the weigh-in scales
the coolers were stacked;
with names on the board
the leaders were jacked.

Weigh In

There were walleyes caught
and a few lake trout,
there were three king salmon
but no brownies weighed out.

Big Brownie was tagged
and lurking the bay,
the reward on his head
the talk of the day.

The End

Glossary

Big Brownie- The Michigan Brown Trout Festival's trophy brown trout tagged for the tournament

bravado- pretended courage or defiant confidence when there is really little or none

brownies- slang for brown trout

buoyed- held up or lifted in spirits or confidence

fret- annoyance or worry

jacked- jacked up, excited

lurking- moving in a concealed or hidden manner

pinged- a bell like sound to warn boats of danger

planer boards- trolling aids used by fishermen to cover more area and reach places unreachable by standard trolling methods

quest- purpose and goal

scurried- busily ran around

tagged- identified with a tag

Big Brownie was made possible by a generous donation from **Alpena Alcona Area Credit Union**, a strong and devoted leader in our community. As an employer, AAACU values its staff and provides competitive wages and benefits to both full and part-time employees.

As a community leader, AAACU focuses on reinvestment, charitable contributions and "people helping people." They help organize fundraisers, charitable events and donate considerable time and money to make a difference in the lives of those around us.

As a not-for-profit cooperative, AAACU is strong, sound and member focused, based on trust and committed to safeguarding member assets. They believe in putting people before money and abide by a strong belief in service above self.

"We are Alpena Alcona Area Credit Union and *everything we do we do for you... the employees, the members and the communities we serve.*"

Almost anyone can experience the AAACU difference! If you live, work or worship in the great state of Michigan you are automatically eligible. Joining is as simple as visiting their website at **aaacu.com** and clicking on "Become a Member."

Learning to save and manage money is also an important asset for children, and can be a fun and informative tool! AAACU's Dollar Dog Kids Club teaches kids ages 12 and younger the value of saving money on a regular basis. Not yet a Dollar Dog Club Member? Visit their website or a branch office to get started.

Alpena Alcona Area Credit Union has offices in Alpena, Atlanta, Lincoln, Oscoda, Ossineke and Tawas City along with three student-run branches located at Alcona High , Alpena High and Oscoda High Schools.

The Michigan Brown Trout Festival

began in 1975. The objective? Catch Big Brownie- a brown trout tagged and let loose in an undisclosed location prior to the festival. Over the years Big Brownie has been caught several times, just not during the tournament.

For 43 years, Big Brownie remained elusive, then, in 2017, Jan Stepanski hooked him during the festival and won a $25,000 prize.

At its core, the Michigan Brown Trout Festival is a series of fishing tournaments, which is appropriate for a city that sits on one of Michigan's Great Lakes- Lake Huron. And in the beginning years, that is pretty much all it was. But over the course of time a small tent was added, then a big tent. Art on the Bay was coordinated to run the same week as Brown Trout. Family Day was added. Teen Night. Tony's Burgers. All this makes the festival one that everyone and anyone can enjoy. It goes without saying, it is now one of the most anticipated events of the summer.

The festival is made possible due to yearlong planning by several service groups. When you attend the festival, any day of the week, you see members of these clubs, as well as our volunteers: keeping the grounds clean, weighing fish, and helping visitors. When the festival ends, they are already working on next year's event.

The committee also receives a great amount of donations from local businesses. Their generosity makes it possible for the community to have the best possible 10 days of fun and excitement.

Thank you for attending the 47th Annual Michigan Brown Trout Festival!! Enjoy all that it has to offer!

For more information visit: **www.browntroutfestival.com**

The author of Big Brownie, Richard Rensberry, is native to the Alpena area. Richard and his wife Mary are co-founders of QuickTurtle Books and Books Make Booms. They write, illustrate and publish books for Michigan small businesses and worthwhile causes. They are proud to be a part of this great Alpena, Michigan tradition.

If you are a business or cause interested in a custom book for your endeavors, please visit: **www.booksmakebooms.com**

The illustrations for this book were painted in oils by wildlife artist Michael Payton. He resides in Colorado Springs, Colorado. You can see more of his work at: **https://1-michael-payton.pixels.com/**

Good Luck!

Made in the USA
Columbia, SC
16 June 2021